Music Genres
Blues Music

by Moira Rose Donohue

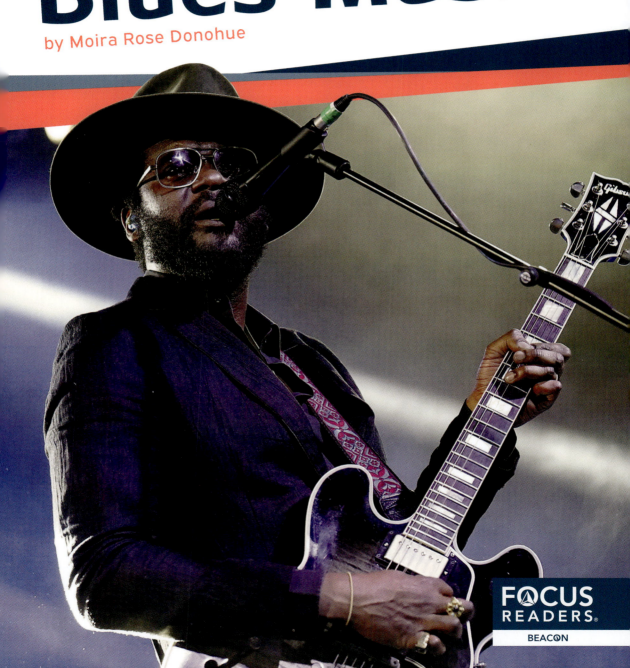

www.focusreaders.com

Copyright © 2025 by Focus Readers®, Mendota Heights, MN 55120. All rights reserved. No part of this book may be reproduced or utilized in any form or by any means without written permission from the publisher.

Focus Readers is distributed by North Star Editions:
sales@northstareditions.com | 888-417-0195

Produced for Focus Readers by Red Line Editorial.

Photographs ©: Acero/Alter Photos/Sipa USA/AP Images, cover, 1; Tim Graham/Alamy, 4; iStockphoto, 6, 8, 11, 29; Shutterstock Images, 12, 18, 22; North Wind Picture Archives/Alamy, 14; Smith Archive/Alamy, 17; Michael Ochs Archives/Getty Images, 20–21; Amy Harris/Invision/AP Images, 25; John Davisson/Invision/AP Images, 26

Library of Congress Cataloging-in-Publication Data
Names: Donohue, Moira Rose, author.
Title: Blues music / by Moira Rose Donohue.
Description: Mendota Heights, MN: Focus Readers, 2025. | Series: Music genres | Includes index. | Audience: Grades 2-3
Identifiers: LCCN 2024003250 (print) | LCCN 2024003251 (ebook) | ISBN 9798889981978 (hardcover) | ISBN 9798889982531 (paperback) | ISBN 9798889983613 (pdf) | ISBN 9798889983095 (ebook)
Subjects: LCSH: Blues (Music)--History and criticism--Juvenile literature.
Classification: LCC ML3521 .D68 2025 (print) | LCC ML3521 (ebook) | DDC 781.64309--dc23/eng/20240123
LC record available at https://lccn.loc.gov/2024003250
LC ebook record available at https://lccn.loc.gov/2024003251

Printed in the United States of America
Mankato, MN
082024

About the Author

Moira Rose Donohue has written more than 40 children's books, including books about tap dance (*Tapping Feet* from Reycraft Books) and drummer Chick Webb (*Stompin' at the Savoy* from Sleeping Bear Press). *Stompin' at the Savoy* won the 2021 Florida Book Award Silver Medal for Young Children's Literature.

Table of Contents

CHAPTER 1
Feeling the Blues 5

CHAPTER 2
What Is Blues Music? 9

CHAPTER 3
Birth of the Blues 15

"Big Mama" Thornton 20

CHAPTER 4
Modern Blues 23

Focus on Blues Music • 28
Glossary • 30
To Learn More • 31
Index • 32

Chapter 1

Feeling the Blues

It's dark and hazy in the theater. The audience is quiet. Everyone is watching the musicians on the stage. One musician raises his electric guitar. His right hand strums the strings.

People often play blues music in theaters, lounges, cafés, and clubs.

 Music can be a way to let out sadness and pain.

His left hand presses some strings down. Sound fills the theater.

The drummer pounds a steady beat. The keyboard player joins in. Then, the guitarist starts to sing. The music is connected to his feelings. The song is sad. The audience thinks about lost loves. People remember lost dreams.

But as the song goes on, feet softly tap. People nod and smile. Somehow, the sad music makes the audience feel better. That's the magic of blues music.

"Having the blues" means feeling sad. That's how blues music got its name.

Chapter 2

What Is Blues Music?

Blues music is often called "the blues." The **genre** is all about feelings. Performers express sadness. They can show it in different ways. For example, musicians use a special **scale**.

In blues music, a song's sounds and words work together to show emotion.

The blues scale has fewer notes compared to scales used in other genres. And the **pitches** of some notes are slightly lower. These are called blue notes. Blues music also uses some common **chord** patterns. For example, many songs switch between three chords.

Most blues songs have lyrics. The words are about heartbreak, hard times, and leaving home. Blues singers use their voices to express these themes. Some artists make

 Some blues songs are about hope and love. But many have themes of pain, loss, and protest.

their voices sound scratchy. Artists may also slide their pitch up or down. Other musicians wail sadly. For instance, blues singer Chester Burnett was known as Howlin' Wolf.

 Some blues artists play the harmonica. They can make notes pulse like a heartbeat.

Burnett used howling sounds to show emotion in his songs.

In blues music, guitar is often the main instrument. Some blues guitars are electric. Others are **acoustic**. Guitarists may use slides.

Slides are hard objects. People move them along the strings. The sound's pitch moves up and down.

Some blues musicians play the string bass. Others plays bass guitar. Drums and keyboard are important, too. Those instruments give blues songs a strong beat.

Did You Know?

B. B. King was a famous blues guitarist. He played several different kinds of guitars. He named them all Lucille.

Chapter 3

Birth of the Blues

Blues is an American genre. But it has African roots. In the 1500s, **enslavers** began capturing people in West Africa. Many people were taken to North America. Enslavers made them do backbreaking work.

 Blues music began with singing. Enslaved people usually didn't have instruments.

Enslaved people often sang as they worked. Some songs were religious. These songs were called spirituals.

Slavery in the United States ended in 1865. Black Americans continued making music. Different areas developed their own sounds. In North Mississippi, some musicians played slide guitar. They made their guitars groan and whine like human voices. The style became the Delta blues. In Texas, musicians picked their

 W. C. Handy (right) was called the "Father of the Blues." He sang with tennis athlete Althea Gibson in 1957.

guitar strings. They sang tunes in high voices. This style became the Texas blues.

In the 1920s, many Black Americans moved north. They hoped for better lives in new cities.

 Many famous blues artists played on Beale Street in Memphis, Tennessee.

That change helped the blues grow. Many musicians stopped in Memphis, Tennessee. They played shows and recorded in **studios**.

Later, many blues musicians went to Chicago, Illinois. B. B. King gained wide audiences there. So did Muddy Waters. Electric guitars gave their music a stronger beat. The blues developed an **urban** sound.

Over time, other subgenres formed. Louis Jordan played the jump blues. It was bouncier and easy to dance to. Cool blues was based on piano.

Beale Street in Memphis, Tennessee, is known as the "Home of the Blues."

ARTIST SPOTLIGHT

"Big Mama" Thornton

Willie Mae "Big Mama" Thornton was born in Alabama in 1926. She taught herself how to play the harmonica. Thornton also wrote and sang songs. She had a special voice. She used a rough style of singing.

In 1952, Thornton recorded a song called "Hound Dog." It sold more than two million copies. Several years later, Elvis Presley recorded the same song. His version became more popular. But Thornton kept performing. She sang the blues for many decades.

"Big Mama" Thornton made only $500 from "Hound Dog."

Chapter 4

Modern Blues

Over the years, the blues became less **mainstream**. But many musicians still played it. And blues helped shape other genres. Jazz musicians drew from the blues. They also added in new chords.

 Jazz is often more upbeat than blues music.

Gospel, country, and rock also grew from the blues. And blues music became the root of today's R&B music.

Over time, the blues also spread to different countries. New styles of blues music developed in those places. For example, artists in the United Kingdom played the British blues. Guitar styles from the British blues inspired many rock musicians. Eric Clapton was one. He became famous across the world.

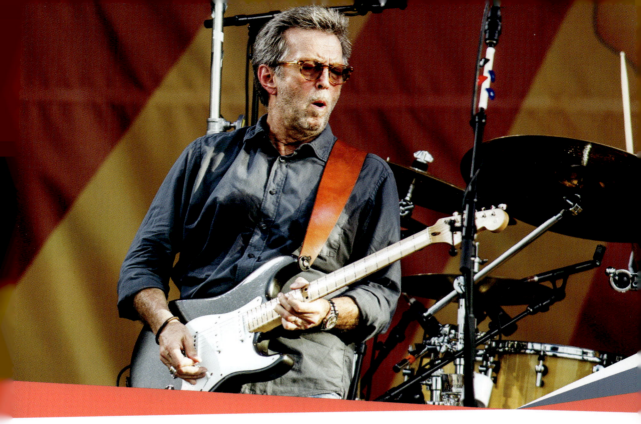

 Eric Clapton is known as one of the greatest guitar players ever.

Today, many blues artists play with **traditional** blues styles. But other artists keep expanding the blues. Guitarist Kenny Wayne Shepherd is one major example.

 By 2024, Gary Clark Jr. had won four Grammy Awards.

Shepherd's music mixes blues with rock. Gary Clark Jr. also blends genres. He uses elements from hip-hop, R&B, and rock music. By mixing genres, these artists have helped the blues find new listeners.

In the 2010s and 2020s, artists of many genres included blues in their music. Listeners around the world enjoyed their work. The power of blues music was still strong. People around the world could express their feelings with the blues.

Did You Know?

Blues music influenced many writers. Langston Hughes is a famous example. Some of his poems sound similar to blues lyrics.

FOCUS ON
Blues Music

Write your answers on a separate piece of paper.

1. Write a few sentences explaining how blues music started.

2. Which common blues instrument would you most want to play? Why?

3. What place is known as the "Home of the Blues"?
    - **A.** North Mississippi
    - **B.** Beale Street in Memphis
    - **C.** the United Kingdom

4. Why might people feel less sad after singing blues songs?
    - **A.** Singing can help let their feelings out.
    - **B.** Singing always makes people happy.
    - **C.** The lyrics of blues songs are not sad.

5. What does **elements** mean in this book?

*Gary Clark Jr. also blends genres. He uses **elements** from hip-hop, R&B, and rock music.*

    A. tastes
    B. sights
    C. sounds

6. What does **version** mean in this book?

*Several years later, Elvis Presley recorded the same song. His **version** became more popular.*

    A. an old style of music
    B. a new form of something
    C. something that is not real

Answer key on page 32.

Glossary

acoustic
Not electric.

chord
A group of notes played at the same time.

enslavers
People who capture other people and force them to work without pay.

genre
A style of music.

mainstream
Popular and known by many people.

pitches
How high or low musical notes are.

scale
A series of musical notes that go up or down.

studios
Rooms or buildings where music is recorded.

traditional
Following practices that have been common in the past.

urban
Relating to a city environment.

To Learn More

BOOKS

Duling, Kaitlyn. *Electric Guitars*. Minneapolis: Bellwether Media, 2023.

Markovics, Joyce. *Muddy Waters*. Ann Arbor, MI: Cherry Lake Publishing, 2024.

Smith, Elliott. *Black Achievements in Music*. Minneapolis: Lerner Publications, 2024.

NOTE TO EDUCATORS

Visit **www.focusreaders.com** to find lesson plans, activities, links, and other resources related to this title.

Index

B
blue notes, 10
Burnett, Chester, 11–12

C
Clapton, Eric, 24
Clark, Gary, Jr., 26

G
guitar, 5–6, 12–13, 16–17, 19, 25

J
Jordan, Louis, 19

K
King, B. B., 13, 18

L
lyrics, 10, 27

M
Mississippi, 16

S
scale, 9–10
Shepherd, Kenny Wayne, 25–26

T
Tennessee, 18–19
Texas, 16–17
Thornton, "Big Mama," 20

W
Waters, Muddy, 19
West Africa, 15

Answer Key: 1. Answers will vary; **2.** Answers will vary; **3.** B; **4.** A; **5.** C; **6.** B